Steps Toward Generosity

Steps Toward Generosity

A 31-Day Journey for Individuals and Church Leaders

Ted W. Nickel

with Sandy Salisbury

Greetings!

Enclosed are a variety of my musings on the topic of generosity.

It is my firm belief, inherited from my father, that church worship should encourage and incorporate generosity on a regular basis. Much emphasis in many churches is placed on singing, almost as though worship and song are one and the same. The act of giving—thoughtfully preparing for and participating in it—is less often called worship. However, I am convinced that giving and being generous of heart is no less worshipful than singing, or indeed than praying, listening to the Word, or fellowshipping together.

Although my name appears here, as I have composed most of these thoughts as talks for church services myself, it is clear to me that almost nothing I say is all that original. I am grateful to the "cloud of witnesses" who have inspired me and educated me over the course of my life.

Ted W. Nickel

Contents

Foreword

It is an honor to introduce these Steps Toward Generosity *written by my friend and colleague, Dr. Ted Nickel. These talks, originally presented in our church, are filled with insight, wisdom, and life perspectives. Sometimes they are accompanied by a touch of gentle humor reminiscent of Ted's father, T. R. Nickel.*

Like their author, these reflections are warmly PERSONAL. They provide real-life lessons and illustrations and do not just proclaim ideals and principles.

They are also INSPIRATIONAL, because the Nickels are known in our congregation as a generous couple; they practice what they preach!

Finally, these short talks are MOTIVATIONAL. They challenge us to reach for higher levels of giving beyond the financial, including the stewardship of friendship, time, and talent.

May you find these reflections on generosity both enjoyable and helpful.

Edmund Janzen
Prof. Emeritus of Biblical and Religious Studies and former president of Fresno Pacific University

Preface

These reflections were prepared by my father for services in his own church, as introductions to the collection. His message was often only a couple of minutes long and concluded with a prayer as the congregation prepared for the offering.

His original compositions have been expanded here so they can be used in multiple ways: as personal devotions, as Bible studies for small groups, as the basis for talks and sermons, and as encouragement for church meetings. Please adapt them to your own use by picking out the best nuggets to introduce the offering or using them as a springboard for further study.

I have been blessed and challenged as I have put this compilation together. Each devotion contains a Scripture passage, two action points, and a summary statement. I have prayed through each devotion and attempted each action point. They are meant to be practical, if not always easy!

I hope you are also blessed and challenged as you take steps toward generosity in your own life. May God inspire your efforts.

Sandy Salisbury

1. Like a Lighthouse

"No one lights a lamp and puts it in a place where it will be hidden, or under a bowl. Instead they put it on its stand, so that those who come in may see the light. Your eye is the lamp of your body. When your eyes are healthy, your whole body also is full of light. But when they are unhealthy, your body also is full of darkness. See to it, then, that the light within you is not darkness. Therefore, if your whole body is full of light, and no part of it dark, it will be just as full of light as when a lamp shines its light on you."

LUKE 11:33–36

Light permeates everything. When I was a boy, I became interested in photography. In those days, processing the film meant setting up a darkroom to turn the negatives into photos. I learned that if the film was exposed to any light before it was taken through a series of chemical baths, the image would be ruined. My dear long-suffering mother allowed me the use of a basement room, and I lined the inside of the doorframe with black tape so there were no gaps around the door when it was shut. It took several layers to block out all the light. Even so, I had to be careful every time I entered the room not to disturb the makeshift barrier. I was impressed by how persistently the light found the smallest gap.

Like a lighthouse, God's generosity to us shines throughout the world and penetrates the darkest places.

We may turn our backs to it, but our shadows will still be proof of the light. When we turn toward the light, we can see clearly.

As God's light shines, it may reveal our own lack of generosity. But as followers of Jesus, we are given the Holy Spirit to help tease out those pockets of darkness.

I have been on the journey toward generosity for a while, and I invite you to join me. Let's allow God's bright light to show us how we can shine with generosity.

When Jesus spoke again to the people, he said, "I am the light of the world. Whoever follows me will never walk in darkness, but will have the light of life."

JOHN 8:12

- Make a list of how God has been generous to you—in gifts of family, friends, health, curiosity, love, humor, wonder, and the beauty around you.
- Determine to take steps toward generosity in your own life as you work through these devotions.

May we all reflect God's generous Spirit.

2. Tithing and Financial Health

People that give ten percent or more are better off financially than those Christians who don't. In every category we measured, faithful and generous giving led to greater financial health in people's lives.

BRIAN KLUTH, *20 TRUTHS ABOUT TITHERS*

What keeps Christians from giving? Brian Kluth's five-year research study, *State of the Plate* (published in 2013), found that most Christians who don't tithe 10 percent of their income claim that either they can't afford to or have too much debt. However, his study goes on to show that those Christians who *do* tithe 10 percent or more of their income are in better health financially.

Is this because those who have more money are more generous? Or is it because those who strive to exercise the gift of generosity find that their financial health improves as a result?

"Bring the whole tithe into the storehouse, that there may be food in my house. Test me in this," says the LORD *Almighty, "and see if I will not throw open the floodgates of heaven and pour out so much blessing that there will not be room enough to store it."*

MALACHI 3:10

God asks us to test Him. *(Us? Test the God of creation?)* In this Old Testament passage, Malachi was speaking at a time when the nation of Israel was struggling financially, and God pinpointed the cause. "You are under a curse—the whole nation—because you are robbing me" (MALACHI 3:9). It was at that point that God challenged them to test Him.

We may not feel able to give 10 percent of our income immediately, but we are all able to make a start. Where can you start?

- Set aside an amount at the beginning of the month, or whenever you receive a paycheck. Don't wait to see if there's anything left over at the end of the month.
- Give to a local organization such as the church where you worship or a Christ-based charity with whom you have a personal connection. You don't have to be restricted by these suggestions, but they're a good starting point.

Now watch for God's blessing, and share it generously!

3. For-give-ness

Why is God's gift of forgiveness so central to being generous?

Let's first consider the word *forgiveness*. The first part, *for*, comes from the Latin prefix *per*, which means "forward, in front of, before, toward." This can refer to future events, as in our words *before* and *forbear*.

If we think of the word *forgive* as "**before**give," it becomes clearer what a gift God is offering.

You see, at just the right time, when we were still powerless, Christ died for the ungodly. Very rarely will anyone die for a righteous person, though for a good person someone might possibly dare to die. But God demonstrates his own love for us in this: While we were still sinners, Christ died for us.

ROMANS 5:6–8

God prepared His gift for us—His Son—before we even thought of asking Him to help us out of our life dilemma. This is a deep spiritual truth at the crux of our relationship with God. He forgave us before we realized we needed forgiveness.

When we accept forgiveness from God, our relationship with Him is restored. And this provides the model for our relationships with others. God forgave us *before* we asked for it, and so we are spurred on to offer the same kind of forgiveness to those around us. Think how much this differs from the usual approach of "I'll only be able to forgive him if he . . ." God's forgiveness is unconditional, radical, and generous!

So, I am thankful for both the pre-emptive strike against my sins that God has provided and how this model guides me toward better relationships.

How can you put this kind of generosity into action?

- Think of someone you see regularly—a family member, a friend, a colleague, a neighbor—who can be annoying sometimes or hard to get along with.
- Determine now to "**before**give" this person. Decide that the next time they do or say something that irritates you, you will let it go. See what a difference this makes to your relationship with them.

Generosity is not just financial; it is also relational.

4. Freedom to Be Generous

Sometimes it feels like we're living dual lives. In our day-to-day activities we are goal-oriented, striving for success and focused on what we can get for ourselves. Complying with the world's stifling standards becomes second nature. Then when we're at church on Sunday morning, we rejoice in the freedom we have through Christ; freedom from the world's expectations. How can we bring this freedom into our everyday lives?

See to it that no one takes you captive through hollow and deceptive philosophy, which depends on human tradition and the elemental spiritual forces of this world rather than on Christ. For in Christ all the fullness of the Deity lives in bodily form, and in Christ you have been brought to fullness. . . .

God made you alive with Christ. He forgave us all our sins, having canceled the charge of our legal indebtedness, which stood against us and condemned us; he has taken it away, nailing it to the cross. And having disarmed the powers and authorities, he made a public spectacle of them, triumphing over them by the cross.

Therefore do not let anyone judge you by what you eat or drink, or with regard to a religious festival, a New Moon celebration or a Sabbath day. These are a shadow of the things that were to come; the reality, however, is found in Christ.

COLOSSIANS 2:8–10,13–17

We are no longer subject to the world's judgment. We are free to be generous: "In Christ [we] have been brought into fullness." Exercising generosity—giving people more time, energy, thought, or money than they deserve—is part of this fullness, part of this freedom.

We will all find different ways to be generous, and that's okay. We don't need to judge others or be constrained by others' judgment, even within the church. We simply need to work at being generous ourselves and encourage each other in our God-given freedom.

- Consider ways in which you put too much emphasis on rules and regulations that prevent you from enjoying the freedom you have in Christ.
- Give someone more time, energy, thought, or money than they deserve, rejoicing in your freedom to be generous!

The reality of our freedom is found in Christ.

5. Financial Sciatica

Were the whole realm of nature mine,
That were a present far too small;
Love so amazing, so divine,
Demands my soul, my life, my all.

ISAAC WATTS, "WHEN I SURVEY THE WONDROUS CROSS"

The sciatic nerve is the largest single nerve in the body. It starts in the lower back and runs through the buttock and down the back of each leg. Portions of the sciatic nerve then branch out in each leg to the thigh, calf, foot, and toes. If this nerve is irritated or pinched in the lower back, it can cause pain all the way down the nerve, sometimes to the toes. A professional will know that addressing sciatic pain in the lower extremities will not solve the problem. They will need to get to the root of the pain—the point at which the nerve is being irritated. And once that problem is resolved, relief comes to the whole body.

"No one can serve two masters. Either you will hate the one and love the other, or you will be devoted to the one and despise the other. You cannot serve both God and money."

LUKE 16:13

Jesus talks about our financial sciatic nerve—that extremely sensitive part of our psyche that is easily pinched. When we are uptight about money, the pain goes through our whole being and we are unable to be generous.

People troubled with sciatica need medical treatment, either from a doctor or chiropractor. When we experience "financial sciatica," we need the treatment of Jesus, the Great Physician. He can address our nerves, heal our ungenerous spirit, and restore it with generosity.

Jesus has done so much for us. He shared His life with us. He invites us into a life of abundance. This doesn't mean that we will become immune to financial challenges, but that those challenges don't need to pinch our generosity.

- Think about your financial situation at the moment. What are your trigger points of pain? Pray through these, and ask Jesus to deal with the other areas of your life that are also affected.
- Thank Jesus for His great generosity toward us.

Let Jesus's spirit of generosity flow through you unhindered.

6. Jesus, Our Coach

Ascribe to the LORD the glory due his name; bring an offering and come before him. Worship the LORD in the splendor of his holiness.

1 CHRONICLES 16:29

In the sporting world, teams rely on the leadership of coaches to perform at their best, and likewise, coaches need the respect of their teams in order to lead effectively. Some coaches are young, quick, and clever. Others have played the game themselves for many years, often in the top leagues, and have won and lost many times. Which kind of coach commands more respect from the team? Undoubtedly the coach with a lot of experience, who has been in the players' position and knows what it takes to succeed on the field.

Our spiritual coach is Jesus, who experienced life in all its many facets. He walked where we walk, felt what we feel, suffered as much as any of us, and then died for us out of His great compassion for our life situations. He has earned our respect. Not only that, but we know that He won. He not only went to the cross and sacrificed His life for us, but He also came back to life, conquering death. He is the winningest coach in history and will lead His team to certain victory over the powers of darkness and death.

We are asked as team members to give our best, our full energy and complete commitment, whether we are on the field or cheering from the stands. No matter our role, we can have full confidence that we are on the winning side.

When we give an offering to the Lord, we are affirming His offering for us. Our contribution may consist of time, talent, money, compassion, or mercy. We can give it joyfully, following the example of our Great Coach.

- Think about your privileged place on Jesus's team. He has a role for you, and you have the opportunity to share in the success of the whole team.
- The next time you give an offering, rejoice that you are part of the worldwide team of God's kingdom.

Jesus's example can coach us in the ways of generosity.

7. The Seventeenth Day of Nisan

The month of Nisan is the first month of the Hebrew calendar and coincides with the beginning of spring—April in the modern Gregorian calendar.

It was the month in which the barley ripened in Israel.

The seventeenth day of the month of Nisan is particularly important in Jewish tradition. Not only does it fall in the middle of the traditional Passover week (celebrated from the fourteenth to the twenty-first of Nisan), but according to the Torah and traditional Jewish interpretation, it was also the day that Noah's ark safely rested on Mount Ararat (Genesis 8:4), the day Moses parted the Red Sea and led the Israelites to safety, (Exodus 5:3, 12:1–20, 14:15,16) and the day Queen Esther saved the Jews from genocide (Esther 3:12, 5:1).

It is also the day when the Israelites, guided by Moses through the wilderness from Egypt, began eating the first fruits of the land of Canaan, the land that God was giving to them.

The people of Israel stayed at Gilgal. They kept the Passover on the evening of the fourteenth day of the first month on the desert plains of Jericho.

On the very next day after the Passover, they ate some of the food of the land. They ate bread without yeast, and dry grain. The bread from heaven stopped on the day after they had eaten some of the food of the land.

So the people of Israel no longer had bread from heaven. But they ate food of the land of Canaan during that year.

JOSHUA 5:10–12 NLV

God had supplied the Israelites with "bread from heaven"—manna—during their journey. But now that they had arrived in the Promised Land, they were no longer dependent on manna. They could enjoy the produce of Canaan. There must have been rejoicing as they tasted the first fruits of their new home!

Most significantly, the seventeenth of Nisan is also the day of the Resurrection. God had planned for Jesus to conquer death on this most important of days. So history comes full circle as God's New Covenant with us through the resurrection of Jesus begins on the anniversary of the ark reaching safety.

- Thank God for his wonderful plan, which is set out in history and culminates in the resurrection of our Lord Jesus Christ.
- Think about a gift you have been given recently: money, food, time, friendship. How can you give back to the Lord some of the firstfruits you have been blessed with?

God's blessings are shown throughout history.

8. Do Not Judge

I was shocked, confused, bewildered
as I entered Heaven's door,
Not by the beauty of it all,
the lights or its decor.

It was the folks in Heaven
who made me sputter and gasp:
the thieves, the liars, the sinners,
the alcoholics and the trash.

There stood the kid from seventh grade
who swiped my lunch money twice.
Next to him was my old neighbor
who never said anything nice.

Herb, who I always thought
was rotting away in hell,
was sitting pretty on cloud nine,
looking incredibly well.

I nudged Jesus, "What's the deal?
I'd love to hear Your take.
How'd all these sinners get up here?
God must've made a mistake.

And why are they so quiet, so somber?
Please give me a clue."
"Hush, child," said He. "They're all in shock.
No one thought they'd see you."

DAVID J. NIXON, "JUDGE NOT"

This is a reflection that brings us all up short!

When we accept what Jesus has done for us, we are freed from being judged. We are also freed from having to judge others. This freedom means that we can give generously without insisting that others account for what they do with our generosity. Let God worry about that!

"Do not judge, and you will not be judged. Do not condemn, and you will not be condemned. Forgive, and you will be forgiven."

LUKE 6:37

- Today, give something to someone who won't have the chance to pay you back (pay for the coffee of the person behind you in the café; drop some coins into the panhandler's hat; provide some company to a housebound neighbor; give a 5-star rating to someone online who didn't ask for it; donate to a small, insignificant charity).
- Commit that gift to God, without worrying about whether it will be used "efficiently" or not.

God's generosity to us is lavishly unconditional.

9. Giving in to "Donor Fatigue"

We often give to a charity because its appeal touches our hearts, it addresses a need that is personal to us, or it conveys a sense of urgency that makes us want to leap into action. However, there are so many worthy charities, and the realization that we can't respond to every one can lead to disillusionment. Eventually, we become convinced that the problems of the world are too big and think, *What difference can my small donation make anyway?*

"Donor fatigue" occurs when otherwise generous individuals start to feel tapped out and unappreciated, hesitating to keep giving when they are inundated with donation requests. They cease to feel invested in their favorite organizations, and they become desensitized to the emotional appeals these organizations make.

However, as Christians, our motivation for being generous is completely different.

When I lived in India for a time, I noticed that the Hindus have a different attitude toward beggars than we have in the West. They seem to relish giving a coin to someone sitting in the street, hands outstretched. When I asked about this, I was told that for Hindus, beggars represent an opportunity to do good, to earn credits so to speak. So the beggar is seen as serving a useful function in society. This gave me a completely different perspective.

A man reaps what he sows. . . . Let us not become weary in doing good, for at the proper time we will reap a harvest if we do not give up. Therefore, as we have opportunity, let us do good to all people, especially to those who belong to the family of believers.

GALATIANS 6:7, 9–10

When we see overwhelming need, it can be tempting to close our hearts and close our wallets. But in his letter to the Galatians, Paul is urging us not to give up. We may not see the end of world poverty in our lifetime, but our generosity is still worthwhile. We give in order to sow for the future, for eternity. And every generous deed will reap its harvest in the end.

- Have you given up on an individual, cause, organization, or challenging situation? Re-evaluate your assessment from God's perspective.
- Commit to making generosity a regular habit that isn't dependent on measurable results.

There will be a great harvest when we sow generously.

10. The New Covenant

When two parties decide to do business together, they draw up a contract. The contract declares the minimum requirements to complete the business transaction, specifying the lowest common denominator that must be fulfilled by each party.

Covenants are different. They state goals, not just responsibilities. They point to the high planes that the parties purpose to achieve. When God entered into a covenant with the nation of Israel, He set down His high purpose for them as His special people. He told Abraham, the father of Israel:

"I will establish my covenant as an everlasting covenant between me and you and your descendants after you for the generations to come, to be your God and the God of your descendants after you. The whole land of Canaan, where you now reside as a foreigner, I will give as an everlasting possession to you and your descendants after you; and I will be their God."

GENESIS 17:7–8

When Jesus came to declare that God's kingdom was to be for all people, He set up a new covenant. As He celebrated the Passover meal with His disciples at the Last Supper, He used the bread and the wine to demonstrate the terms of this new covenant. He picked up a cup of wine and said, "This cup is the new covenant in my blood, which is poured out for you" (LUKE 22:20).

This new covenant was no longer limited to the people of Israel but was freely available to the whole world. The terms of the covenant are found in Jesus's actions. He poured out His life for us, holding nothing back.

That is the goal to which we aspire. As Jesus gave freely of Himself, let's determine to give freely of ourselves to others when we see a need.

- Ask God to help you be sensitive to the needs of others.
- When you see someone in need this week, stop and help them without worrying about whether your resources are sufficient. Trust God to be sufficient for you.

God's covenant to us is limitless in its generosity.

11. The Right Decision

"So do not worry, saying, 'What shall we eat?' or 'What shall we drink?' or 'What shall we wear?' For the pagans run after all these things, and your heavenly Father knows that you need them. But seek first his kingdom and his righteousness, and all these things will be given to you as well."

MATTHEW 6:31–33

How do you make good decisions? How do you know whether the decision you have made is right? What if doing the other thing would have been better?

So often we are paralyzed by the decision that confronts us: which course to study, which job to apply for, where to live, how to use our money wisely, whom to marry, how to solve a family dispute. These are decisions that will likely have long-lasting implications. What if we make the wrong decision? Will our lives be ruined?

I was struck by something I heard many years ago, and it has guided my decision-making ever since. A wise fellow told me to "make a decision, then make it right." His wisdom was that though we may not know which option is the best, we should work hard *after* the decision has been reached to make the best of what we have decided. In most situations, God is not as concerned with *what* we decide as with *how* we handle the results of our decision.

Jesus decided to come down to earth and live a human life among us. This decision foreshadowed a future that would bring Him great agony, but He made it right. Many who witnessed Him dying on the cross, even His followers, thought He had made the wrong decision. But Jesus's resurrection showed that even the direst of circumstances can result in victory if we allow God's glory to shine through.

- Think about a difficult decision you have to make in the near future. Consider your options in a spirit of generosity, pray about it, and then make your decision.
- After you've made the decision, don't spend time worrying about what might have been, but allow God to help you make the decision right.

God is more interested in helping us make our decisions right than in punishing us for "wrong" decisions.

12. Bring Encouragement

"It was the best of times, it was the worst of times . . ." Charles Dickens opened his great novel *A Tale of Two Cities* with that famous line. I will instead tell you the tale of two payments.

One of my responsibilities in my church is to be the second authorizer of payments. Someone else initiates the payments, and they are passed to me to check them over. Recently, there were two payments to make on the same day: one for the work of the children's ministries and the other for the expenses of "Meal and More," our monthly community event.

I really enjoyed approving the payment for the children's ministries. Putting the church's resources toward teaching children about God's love for them and guiding them to live their lives well is such a good investment. The second payment was for food and equipment. As I thought about it, this was also an investment: an investment in the community. People who don't normally come to our Sunday morning services feel comfortable enough to come on a weeknight to receive a meal—and hopefully some spiritual food too.

Beyond the obvious benefit of providing the practical resources needed, monetary donations also validate the church or charity workers in their roles. For those who work to organize our church events, take part in running projects for the community, and give of their time to support others in need, financial donations are such a boost.

Therefore encourage one another and build each other up, just as in fact you are doing. Now we ask you, brothers and sisters, to acknowledge those who work hard among you, who care for you in the Lord and who admonish you. Hold them in the highest regard in love because of their work. Live in peace with each other.

1 THESSALONIANS 5:11–13

So when we feel blessed in "the best of times," we can encourage those who minister to people who may be experiencing "the worst of times."

- Think about an individual or group working in a special ministry within your local church or a charity that means something to you.
- Pray for them, let them know that you're praying for them, and think about how you can support them in their ministry.

Show your regard for church and charity workers.

13. The Password

Nowadays, we have PINs or passwords for everything—and keeping track of them is a major hassle. The Psalms tell us that there is just one password to God: Thanks.

I will give thanks to you forever for what you have done. In the presence of your godly people, I will wait with hope in your good name.

PSALM 52:9 GW

It is good to give thanks to the LORD, to make music to praise your name, O Most High.

PSALM 92:1 GW

Thanksgiving opens up our hearts to God. It allows God to enter our lives. It focuses us on what is truly important in life. Let us continually give thanks.

But it doesn't end with giving thanks. Our thanksgiving leads us to take action. One of my father's favorite sayings was "Sympathy without relief is like mustard without beef." It reminds us that our words, although important, are insufficient if they're not followed up with actions. If a friend is in trouble, it's great to encourage them and offer a sympathetic word. But it's even better to offer practical help.

As we gain access to God's resources and power by using the password of "thanks," we are enabled to do good works, make good decisions, and meet our daily challenges. Giving thanks equips us for the tasks ahead.

It strengthens us to work for the good of others, knowing how blessed we are.

- As you go about your usual tasks today, give thanks at every opportunity. Let your actions be powered by the resources God gives you.
- The next time you hear of a friend's trouble, give thanks for the opportunity given to you by God to minister, and then take action. Even a small gesture will be a blessing.

Giving thanks helps us tap into God-given resources.

14. Jet Lag

If you've taken a long-haul flight, you know that feeling. Your body clock says it's time to sleep and yet it's the middle of the day at your destination. Everyone around you is eating lunch, but you have no appetite. Later, in the dead of the night, you find yourself wide awake—and likely peckish. It can take some time to adjust to the new time zone.

Of course, a similar feeling results from taking part in all-night parties or caring for sleep-averse babies. Whichever you've experienced, that fuzzy-headed feeling accompanied by leaden limbs is the body's way of protesting our capricious time-keeping.

Jesus went into Galilee, proclaiming the good news of God. "The time has come," he said. "The kingdom of God has come near. Repent and believe the good news!"

MARK 1:14–15

Jesus was talking about a new time zone. If we are trying to follow Jesus but live by the world's time, we will fall out of step with the kingdom of God and experience "spiritual jet lag."

The Gospel of Luke gives a fuller account of Jesus's declaration. He quotes from the prophet Isaiah to explain what the time zone of God's kingdom looks like.

"The Spirit of the Lord is on me, because he has anointed me to proclaim good news to the poor. He has sent me to proclaim freedom for the prisoners and recovery of sight

for the blind, to set the oppressed free, to proclaim the year of the Lord's favor. . . . Today this scripture is fulfilled in your hearing."

LUKE 4:18, 21

Generosity toward the poor, the imprisoned, the blind, and the oppressed is normal in God's time zone but not the world's time zone. Let's reset our spiritual clocks. *Today* is the day that Jesus brings in the new order. Don't be dragged down by the old time zone any longer.

- Think of a situation in which you find it particularly difficult to be generous. Ask God to help you change your mind-set.
- Show by practical action that you are living according to God's time in this situation.

Be released into the time zone of God's kingdom.

15. Delay of Gratification

In 1962, psychology professor Walter Mischel devised an experiment that has come to be known as the Marshmallow Test. In the Stanford University nursery, he presented preschoolers with a choice: either have one treat now (their favorite candy or cookie) or have two treats later. Mischel recorded the results and studied these children as they grew up. It became clear that the choice they had made as young children was a very good indicator of their future success in adulthood. If they had chosen to wait for two treats, they could be predicted to do better in school, get better exam results, have more successful careers, and even save up more effectively for their retirement.

Saint Paul urges us to have the same attitude as Christ:

Who, being in very nature God, did not consider equality with God something to be used to his own advantage; rather, he made himself nothing by taking the very nature of a servant, being made in human likeness. And being found in appearance as a man, he humbled himself by becoming obedient to death— even death on a cross! Therefore God exalted him to the highest place and gave him the name that is above every name.

PHILIPPIANS 2:6–9

Jesus could have assumed the role of King of kings when He came to earth; the devil even confirmed this when he tried to tempt Jesus to take a position of power (Matthew 4:8–11). But Jesus resisted the temptation, knowing that He would face poverty, scorn, and eventually a criminal's death. But He also knew that the result of His sacrifice would be His ultimate triumph over death and the redemption of humankind. He was willing to forego present comforts for future glory.

Professor Mischel explains in his book, *The Marshmallow Test*, that the skill of delayed gratification can be taught, and it is one of the greatest gifts a parent can give their children.

The discipline of regular giving helps us practice delayed gratification. We deny ourselves the brief pleasure of what money can buy for us now in the knowledge that God will multiply the gift for future glory.

- The next time you reach for a treat—a chocolate bar, a latté, an on-demand video rental—resist just this once and put the equivalent amount aside for your offering.
- Remember children who are close to you in your prayers, and pray that God will help them develop this important skill.

"If we hope for what we do not yet have, we wait for it patiently" (ROMANS 8:25).

16. God's Handiwork

"Welcome. And congratulations. I am delighted that you could make it. Getting here wasn't easy, I know. In fact, I suspect it was a little tougher than you realize. To begin with, for you to be here now trillions of drifting atoms had somehow to assemble in an intricate and intriguingly obliging manner to create you. It's an arrangement so specialized and particular that it has never been tried before and will only exist this once. For the next many years (we hope) these tiny particles will uncomplainingly engage in all the billions of deft, cooperative efforts necessary to keep you intact and let you experience the supremely agreeable but generally underappreciated state known as existence. Why atoms take this trouble is a bit of a puzzle."

BILL BRYSON, *THE SHORT HISTORY OF NEARLY EVERYTHING*

But we do know why atoms take this trouble: They are ordered by God. It is a miracle. It is not only the miracle of life but also the miracle of free will, of personal choice.

Atoms, which are in themselves lifeless, are formed together by God's Spirit to create you: a living, breathing, animated being that chooses. The choices you make of your own free will are what make you who you are.

You can choose to work with God in His creation, to help His kingdom come. You can choose to worship Him and put Him in the right place in your life. And you can choose to honor Him by offering yourself to Him.

For you created my inmost being; you knit me together in my mother's womb. I praise you because I am fearfully and wonderfully made; your works are wonderful, I know that full well.

PSALM 139:13–14

For we are God's handiwork, created in Christ Jesus to do good works, which God prepared in advance for us to do.

EPHESIANS 2:10

- Thank God for how wonderfully He created you in your complexity. Thank Him for your uniqueness and for giving you gifts that He has given no one else in the same combination.
- Think of one of your special gifts—you could ask a friend to help you discern this—and commit that gift to being used for God.

Your uniqueness is a great gift.

17. Opposites

Take a look at your hand. Which finger is the most beautiful? The ring finger? The little one? You are unlikely to pick the thumb, but consider another situation.

A ruthless dictator has arrested you for some infraction and threatens to have one of your fingers chopped off. He will choose which finger, but you may protect one. Which one will you protect? The most sensible choice is the thumb. Why? Because this opposable digit makes your hand much more useful.

What's your favorite color? Not many people would choose black, and yet that is the color (or achromatic color) most used in art and printing. Look at this page. The blank ink contrasts best with the white page, making it easy for you to read. After the printing press was invented, printers searched for the blackest ink they could find and discovered that mixing soot, turpentine and walnut oil produced the most brilliant black. They valued how it made the print stand out on white sheets of paper.

Those who give to the poor will lack nothing, but those who close their eyes to them receive many curses.

PROVERBS 28:27

Jesus taught that "it is more blessed to give than to receive" (Acts 20:35). This contrasts sharply with how most people feel. I like to receive things, and it is human nature to spend a lot of our time trying to acquire. But that verse from Proverbs, and Jesus's words, teach that in order to be open to receiving, you must give.

Frankly, God doesn't need anything we could give Him; He already owns everything. But when we give, something very powerful happens. It creates the opportunity for us to receive. We appreciate the value of receiving much more when we give. The act of giving puts the joy of receiving in sharp relief, like black ink on a white page. And just as our opposable thumbs help us grasp objects more firmly, giving helps us grasp the significance of receiving more profoundly. And so, in the opposites we find blessing.

- Look for other opposites in nature and in life. How does their contrast enhance the world?
- Give an offering this week without expecting to receive. And then, open up your mind to how many ways you receive from God.

Opposites are part of the wonder of God's creation.

18. The Greatest Multiplier

John Maynard Keynes, one of the most influential economists in modern times, introduced the concept of the "Spending Multiplier." This phenomenon is used by governments to boost the economy.

The Spending Multiplier says that if the government injects a certain amount of cash into the economy, the result will be an increase in overall spending by a multiple of that amount. This is because individuals will save some and spend the rest. Whatever is spent becomes someone else's income, which they will spend toward another person's income, which that person will spend, and so on. This is known as the "ripple effect." The initial injection of government money is spent over and over, stimulating the economy and "creating" more wealth for everyone (in an ideal world, disregarding inflation, borrowing, varying exchange rates, corruption, and other pitfalls).

In God's economy, whatever you give will be multiplied many times over, without any pitfalls. I have seen this in my local church. For many years, we have supported the work of people going out into other parts of the world. Our church is small, and the amount we have donated isn't particularly significant. And yet, these people come back from time to time and give testimonies of how God is working in these countries. In southern Asia, the churches we have been helping to support now have over 40,000 members. This staggers me.

We are very small, but God can use the little we give and multiply it many times. I am so thankful.

Then Peter stood up with the Eleven, raised his voice and addressed the crowd. . . . "Repent and be baptized, every one of you, in the name of Jesus Christ for the forgiveness of your sins. And you will receive the gift of the Holy Spirit. . . ." With many other words he warned them; and he pleaded with them, "Save yourselves from this corrupt generation." Those who accepted his message were baptized, and about three thousand were added to their number that day.

ACTS 2:14, 38, 40–41

Twelve disciples brought the Good News to Jerusalem on that first Pentecost, and by the end of the day there were over 3,000 followers of Jesus. What a multiplier!

- Consider the amount you put aside regularly for the work of God's church. Thank God that He *will* multiply your gift for His kingdom.
- Do a little research on where your giving goes and the results that can be measured.

God's economy out-performs the world's.

19. Speeding Down the Highway

Do you remember learning to ride a bicycle? I learned when I was five or six years old, and I still remember the bruised elbows, the scraped knees, and then that incredible moment when I was finally on my own, the wind in my face, the world flashing by, balanced for once.

When I was about twelve, I determined to learn how to ride my bicycle while sitting backward on the handlebars. That required me to peddle backward and steer backward—the complete opposite of what I'd learned before. This made me realize that there are two skills to riding a bicycle that are counterintuitive.

First, you have to have speed. The slower you pedal, the more danger there is of falling. With speed comes stability. My friends and I would sometimes have races to see who could cross the finish line *last* without falling off their bike. Cycling slowly makes it much more difficult to stay balanced.

Second, when you start to fall, you have to steer in the direction of the fall. This is the hardest thing to do because every fiber in your body wants to turn away from the fall. But if you steer into it, you can get the bike back under you and correct yourself.

Each of you should give what you have decided in your heart to give, not reluctantly or under compulsion, for God loves a cheerful giver. And God is able to bless you abundantly, so that in all things at all times, having all that you need, you will abound in every good work. As it is written:

"They have freely scattered their gifts to the poor; their righteousness endures forever."

Now he who supplies seed to the sower and bread for food will also supply and increase your store of seed and will enlarge the harvest of your righteousness. You will be enriched in every way so that you can be generous on every occasion, and through us your generosity will result in thanksgiving to God.

2 CORINTHIANS 9:7–11

Giving money away is counterintuitive; it goes against the grain. But the more we do it, the more momentum we build up and the easier (and more rewarding) it becomes. And if we start to fall, we simply need to continue giving, trusting God. These words from Corinthians promise us that the more we give, the more God will increase our capacity to give.

- If you haven't already, set up a regular donation—weekly or monthly—so that you can maintain your giving momentum.
- Make a small increase to your regular donation and see how God honors it.

Maintain your generosity momentum.

20. The Cargo Cult

The islanders of the South Pacific had little contact with Western society until the nineteenth century. Suddenly, ships started arriving carrying bounty that the islanders had not previously known. They thought their gods were blessing them.

During World War II, the Allies and the Japanese set up airbases throughout the South Pacific, sometimes right next to villages. The islanders observed aircraft arriving with loads of food, arms, and wealth. When these airbases were abandoned after the war, villagers attempted to get cargo to fall from the sky again by imitating the appearance and behavior of the airmen they'd observed: dressing as soldiers, parading across the landing strips, wearing mock headphones carved from wood, and waving landing signals on the runways.

Charismatic individuals in the villages would set themselves up as leaders of these "cargo cults," promising their followers untold riches from the skies. They turned military practices into worship rituals. It isn't clear if these leaders were sincere or simply running scams on gullible locals.

As far as the locals were concerned, their gods were being generous to them, but they didn't know why or how and their gods weren't always reliable. Sometimes the cargo arrived and sometimes it didn't.

"Do not judge, and you will not be judged. Do not condemn, and you will not be condemned. Forgive, and

you will be forgiven. Give, and it will be given to you. A good measure, pressed down, shaken together and running over, will be poured into your lap. For with the measure you use, it will be measured to you."

LUKE 6:37–38

Jesus tells us exactly how and why blessings are given to us by God. We are aware of and receive blessings to the extent that we give. If we are miserly, we won't recognize God's blessings for what they are. If we are generous, we will see God's blessings poured down on us and running over.

Jesus also teaches that giving generously is not limited to money. It also includes being generous with our judgment of others, our acceptance of others who do things differently, and our forgiveness of others.

- Be generous in your acceptance of someone who is different. Don't withhold your welcome from a newcomer.
- Praise God for the ways in which He fills our lives to overflowing with blessings.

God is the one true, reliable source of all our blessings.

21. Sink Your Plow

He who serves a revolution plows the sea.

SIMÓN BOLIVAR

Simon Bolivar (1783–1830) is considered the father of Hispanic America. He dreamed of a united Spanish America, and in the pursuit of that purpose, he fought for and won independence from Spain for modern-day Venezuela, Colombia, Ecuador, Peru, and Bolivia (named after him). However, Bolivar ultimately failed to hold these countries together in a Confederation of the Andes and saw his dream of democratic republics being replaced by dictatorships as he lay dying of tuberculosis. In frustration he penned a letter to his friend, General Juan José Flores, head of the state of Ecuador, describing his achievements as "plowing the sea."

To spend your energy and resources plowing the sea is the ultimate picture of futility. It is a worthless pursuit. Jesus says:

"'No one who puts a hand to the plow and looks back is fit for service in the kingdom of God.'" . . . After this the Lord appointed seventy-two others and sent them two by two ahead of him to every town and place where he was about to go. He told them, "The harvest is plentiful, but the workers are few. Ask the Lord of the harvest, therefore, to send out workers into his harvest field."

LUKE 9:62, 10:2

Jesus tells His followers to plow. He tells them to plow with determination and without hesitation because the harvest is plentiful. If we plow where Jesus shows us, it will not be a worthless pursuit.

The difference between how Bolivar was plowing and how Jesus's followers plow is not so much their commitment and energy level as the ground in which the plow is sunk. Plowing into rich, dark, fertile soil yields a far greater harvest than plowing into barren sand, so putting our resources and energy into building God's kingdom yields much more than the pursuit of purely political aims.

Bolivar achieved a lot, but his results did not lead to permanent freedom and democracy throughout Hispanic America. However, the investments we make in God's kingdom will return benefits for eternity. Plowing is good, honest, hard work. Make sure you are plowing the right field.

- Explore the areas you put the most energy and resources into. Are they suitable places to sink your plow?
- Thank God that He is using your generosity for eternal benefits, even if you can't see the harvest yet.

Jesus promises a plentiful harvest for those who sink their plows into His fields.

22. Good Circulation

I recently installed a closed-circuit TV system in our community RV parking lot. This involved putting up thirty-foot poles in each of the four corners, fixing cameras to the top of them, hooking them up with lots of wiring, and connecting them to an electricity source. My first test of the system was unsuccessful, but I finally determined that I hadn't connected the return wires properly in order to make a functioning electrical circuit. Although electricity had been going to the cameras, it had no way out without the return wires and, therefore, couldn't flow.

The same principle applies to lakes. For a lake to function properly, it needs to have a water outlet as well as a water inlet. We all know that the Dead Sea is so named because fish can't live in it. It has no outlet, so the water becomes stagnant and unable to sustain life. What a contrast to the beautiful, life-sustaining waters of Lake Victoria on the Nile, or Lake Superior on the St. Marys River, Loch Lomond on the Falloch, and Lake Tahoe on the Truckee River.

Jesus stood and said in a loud voice, "Let anyone who is thirsty come to me and drink. Whoever believes in me, as Scripture has said, rivers of living water will flow from within them."

JOHN 7:37–38

Jesus talks a lot about the dangers of clinging too tightly to earthly goods. They can stick to us and act as a dam, preventing His living water from flowing.

Jesus promises to give us all that we need. If we are thirsty, He will give us living water to drink. Our natural response should be to allow that living water to flow through us and out to those around us.

Let's open up the channels and allow God's rich blessings to flow from us to others.

- Think of a material object you value highly: your house, car, tablet or other electronic device, a kitchen appliance, a piece of furniture, a flat-screen television or sound system. Ask God how you can use this object to bless others. Perhaps host someone in difficulty, give someone a lift, cook a meal for someone who can't get out, or let someone borrow your tools.
- Keep this attitude in mind the next time you buy something new or receive something as a gift.

The key to an object's worth is its circulation capacity.

23. Ask Well

Where do you think your fighting and endless conflict come from? Don't you think that they originate in the constant pursuit of gratification that rages inside each of you like an uncontrolled militia? You crave something that you do not possess, so you murder to get it. You desire the things you cannot earn, so you sue others and fight for what you want. You do not have because you have chosen not to ask. And when you do ask, you still do not get what you want because your motives are all wrong – because you continually focus on self-indulgence.

You are adulterers. Don't you know that making friends with this corrupt world order is open aggression toward God? So anyone who aligns with this bogus world system is declaring war against the one true God. Do you think it is empty rhetoric when the Scriptures say, "The spirit that lives in us is addicted to envy and jealousy"?

You may think that the situation is hopeless, but God gives us more grace when we turn away from our own interests. That's why Scripture says, "God opposes the proud, but He pours out grace on the humble."

JAMES 4:1–6 THE VOICE

It is so difficult to separate our needs from our wants and pray with the right motives. In this Scripture passage, James is very blunt. Within each of us is the capacity to do harm to others because of selfish desire. Our lack of generosity is a trait common to all people.

But the situation is not hopeless, says James. We just need to turn away from our own interests. Then God will be generous toward us in His grace and will shower us with the desire to be generous to others.

"Ask and it will be given to you; seek and you will find; knock and the door will be opened to you."

MATTHEW 7:7

Jesus encourages us to ask Him for what we need! He loves when we come to Him with our prayers. The key is the spirit in which we make our requests to Him. We need to first put aside our selfish interests and listen to God's interests.

- Instead of praying, "please can I have . . .", start your prayers with "please show me what You desire." Then spend a little time listening and allowing God to show you His grace.
- Finish your prayers by asking God to help you be faithful and generous with what He has already given you.

Asking well means listening first.

24. Study the Right Source

For millennia, many people believed the earth was flat. After all, what they could see of the world ended at the horizon, and when boats sailed past the horizon, they often didn't come back. The theory kept people sailing close to shore, which kept them safer from storms at sea because they were able to get to a harbor quickly in bad weather. However, astronomers such as Eratosthenes and Galileo determined from their studies of the sun and stars that the earth is spherical.

The flat earth theory was useful up to a point, but it was wrong, and learning that the earth is round has enabled us to travel farther, trade more, and judge the weather better, among other things.

For many years, people thought that ulcers were caused by stress and eating spicy food. The answer according to this theory was to stop eating curry and drink lots of milk. In 1981, intern doctor Barry Marshall teamed up with pathologist Robin Warren at the Royal Perth Hospital in Australia and found that Helicobacter pylori bacteria were responsible for up to 85 percent of ulcers as well as some stomach cancers. The medical establishment was reluctant to accept this new theory, so Marshall actually experimented on himself by drinking a concoction containing the suspect bacteria. He quickly developed an ulcer, which he treated with antibiotics. For their work on Helicobacter pylori, Marshall and Warren shared a 2005 Nobel Prize. Today the standard treatment for an ulcer is antibiotics. And stomach cancer, once one of the most common forms of malignancy, is almost gone from the Western world.

The ancient astronomers and the ulcer doctors both focused their studies on the *source* rather than the residual effects of the phenomenon.

The beginning of wisdom is this: Get wisdom. Though it cost all you have, get understanding. . . . The fear of the LORD *is the beginning of wisdom, and knowledge of the Holy One is understanding.*

PROVERBS 4:7, 9:10

God is our source. We will gain wisdom by studying Him. When we face problems, whether they are financial, relational, practical, or spiritual, the best thing we can do is start by focusing on the Lord.

- What problem do you face at the moment? Look to God first before you search for a solution.

- Remember that "if any of you lacks wisdom, you should ask God, who gives generously to all without finding fault, and it will be given to you" (JAMES 1:5).

Look to the Source for wisdom.

25. A Collective Offering

"What's in a name? That which we call a rose, By any other name would smell as sweet."

In these famous lines from Shakespeare's *Romeo and Juliet*, Juliet bemoans the fact that because Romeo comes from the Montague family (the rival of her Capulet clan) they cannot marry. She wonders why a name should be so important.

But the Bible puts a lot of importance on names. Jesus renamed his disciple Simon as Peter, meaning "Rock," and declared, "And I tell you that you are Peter, and on this rock I will build my church, and the gates of Hades will not overcome it" (MATTHEW 16:18).

The apostle Paul was also called Saul. Saul was his original Hebrew name, and Paul was his name as a Roman citizen. It was typical for the Jews of that time to have two names: one Hebrew, the other Latin or Greek. Paul used his Roman name when interacting with the Gentile world. His strategy was to put people at their ease and approach them with his message in a language they could relate to.

Throughout the Bible, God is given many names to remind us of His attributes: *Elohim* (Sovereign), *Yahweh* (I Am), *Abba* (Father), *El Shaddai* (All Powerful), *Yahwah Yireh* (God Will Provide), *Jehovah Rapha* (The Lord Heals), and many more.

We use collective nouns to describe animal groups. A group of sheep is called a flock, crows comprise a murder, and several porcupines is a prickle. Have you seen a tower of giraffes or a crash of rhinoceroses? Perhaps you have been bothered by an intrusion of cockroaches.

These collective names point to an attribute of the animals. What collective name would the followers of Jesus best be known by?

Ascribe to the LORD, all you families of nations, ascribe to the LORD glory and strength. Ascribe to the LORD the glory due his name; bring an offering and come into his courts.

PSALM 96:7–8

The psalmist calls on all God's followers to bring an offering. Perhaps "offering" would be an appropriate collective name for Christians? Let's strive to live up to it.

- How can you show today that you are part of the collective offering of Christians?
- Be encouraged by stories of generosity from Christians from around the world. Go to givewithjoy.org/true_stories.htm.

Make "offering" part of your name.

26. Doorkeepers

Many people give to a church or charity when they hear a deserving appeal or when something happens in their lives to prompt them to give a generous offering. Some people set up regular payments from their bank account or set aside a regular amount from their income to put into the offering basket.

What are the benefits of regular giving? Why set aside an amount to give if there is no specific appeal for funds at the moment?

The book of Chronicles gives a lot of detail on the running of the kingdoms of Israel and Judah. We read the names of all the kings and top advisers. But 1 Chronicles 26 also lists the doorkeepers, or gatekeepers, of the temple by name and their family lines.

These divisions of the gatekeepers, through their leaders, had duties for ministering in the temple of the LORD, just as their relatives had. . . . The lot for the East Gate fell to Shelemiah. Then lots were cast for his son Zechariah, a wise counselor, and the lot for the North Gate fell to him. The lot for the South Gate fell to Obed-Edom, and the lot for the storehouse fell to his sons. . . . These were the divisions of the gatekeepers who were descendants of Korah and Merari.

1 CHRONICLES 26:12, 14–15, 19

What's so important about doorkeepers that their names are recorded in Scripture? They were responsible for reminding the people of their spiritual and practical duties in the temple. They guarded the temple area and watched who went in and out. It was a humble yet vital job. Remember the psalmist's words: "I would rather be a doorkeeper in the house of my God than dwell in the tents of the wicked" (PSALM 84:10).

Doorkeepers are the first to hear news; they control what comes in and goes out. They regulate trade. In our lives, regulating what comes in and goes out is vital. Keeping a regular watch on our finances—what comes in and goes out—is part of being a follower of Christ. Setting up a regular payment to our church or chosen charity keeps the flow of generosity going.

- If you haven't already, organize a regular payment to your church or chosen charity, either through a bank account or by setting aside a specific amount each week or month.
- Be a good doorkeeper: check your finances on a regular basis—at least monthly—and thank God every time you come across your regular donation in your accounts.

Doorkeepers are vital in God's kingdom.

27. Well Taught

I love proverbs. You know, when people say, "Absence makes the heart grow fonder," or "Out of sight, out of mind." How about "Birds of a feather flock together" and "Opposites attract"? Are they both true? If so, they seem to contradict each other. Of course, they can both be true in certain contexts.

"Experience is the best teacher." That is a popular proverb, but if it is always true then I am out of a job, because I am a teacher. I believe it can be true in some contexts, such as when children first learn to walk. They pull themselves up, then fall down. Then they pull themselves up again, balance for a bit, and fall down. Eventually, their experience of falling down teaches them how to balance on their feet reliably. Parents don't "teach" their children to walk so much as provide the right environment in which they can learn safely.

However, in many other areas of life, experience comes at far too high a cost. It is one thing to fall six inches onto a soft floor. It is another altogether to have a head-on collision as a new driver because no one told you that you should stay on your side of the road. Driving is a skill with a dangerous learning curve and needs to be taught.

I am grateful to the many people who, down through the years, taught me about life and saved me from learning purely from experience. I am glad that someone told me not to smoke as a youngster. Of course, people tried to teach me other things that I went on to learn the hard way.

Dedicate your children to God and point them in the way that they should go, and the values they've learned from you will be with them for life.

PROVERBS 22:6 TPT

The best thing you can do for your children is train them well. You may not be a professional teacher, but you can lead them by example. Being generous is a powerful example to children—both your own and other children in your community. I don't believe the verse from Proverbs is limited to nuclear families. We can all be an example to the young people around us. Let your life radiate generosity, following Christ's example, for the benefit of the next generation.

- Think about children and young people in your immediate circle. Pray that they will learn good values.
- When the opportunity arises, explain to a young person why you have been generous in a specific situation. With humility!

Be a generous example.

28. Stop Grumbling

We love to complain. Conversations are often based on the rising cost of fuel and food, the bad state of the roads, the shocking level of government corruption, or the weather. This has always been the case.

All the People of Israel grumbled against Moses and Aaron. The entire community was in on it: "Why didn't we die in Egypt? Or in this wilderness? Why has GOD brought us to this country to kill us? Our wives and children are about to become plunder. Why don't we just head back to Egypt? . . ."

GOD spoke to Moses and Aaron: "How long is this going to go on, all this grumbling against me by this evil-infested community? I've had my fill of complaints from these grumbling Israelites. Tell them, As I live—GOD's decree—here's what I'm going to do: Your corpses are going to litter the wilderness—every one of you twenty years and older who was counted in the census, this whole generation of grumblers and grousers. Not one of you will enter the land and make your home there, the firmly and solemnly promised land, except for Caleb son of Jephunneh and Joshua son of Nun."

NUMBERS 14:1–3, 26–30 MSG

The Israelites thought they had good reason to grumble. Their scouts had just returned with news of the ferocious enemies occupying the land God had promised to them. But instead of focusing on God's promises, they focused on the obstacles. The consequence was that they didn't get to enjoy the results of His blessings; the Promised Land was given to the next generation.

We all face many obstacles in life and can so easily be pulled down into grumbling. Sometimes we need a change of perspective. That loaf of bread may be more expensive this month, but it still costs a fraction of the man-hours it would have cost our grandparents. Ill health may drag you down, but medical care is so much better and more humane than it was in previous generations. We have a lot to be thankful for.

The Israelites had forgotten that God had released them from the misery of slavery in Egypt. God's generosity continues to be boundless. Don't miss out on it by grumbling.

- How has life improved compared to previous generations? Think of your own examples.
- The next time you are tempted to complain or are dragged into a grumbler's conversation, try shifting the focus to thankfulness.

Let thankfulness overcome grumbling.

29. FOMO

Fear of missing out (FOMO) is becoming a widespread phenomenon in the social media age. If we're not connected to the cyber universe 24/7, we may feel that we'll miss out on something crucial. Social media apps fuel this fear by feeding us flashy ads for things we "need" to buy. The FOMO Fashion website promises, "We got you, girl! Never miss a new arrival or exclusive promotion again!" There's even a FOMO music festival in Australia, where all the bands play on a single stage so attendees won't miss what might be happening elsewhere.

People are realizing that this is a serious problem. FOMO threatens relationships and mental well-being. A science has built up around helping people who suffer from this "new virus." Google is responding to worries about FOMO by introducing apps that will "bring about disconnection by giving people information that helps them reflect upon their own usage and digital behaviors and the tools to disconnect." I wonder how successful using apps to treat an app addiction will be!

FOMO was officially added to the Oxford English Dictionary in 2013, but it's nothing the world hasn't seen before. Listen to Jesus:

"If God gives such attention to the appearance of wildflowers—most of which are never even seen—don't you think he'll attend to you, take pride in you, do his best for you? What I'm trying to do here is to get you to relax, to not be so preoccupied with getting, so you can respond

to God's giving. People who don't know God and the way he works fuss over these things, but you know both God and how he works. Steep your life in God-reality, God-initiative, God-provisions. Don't worry about missing out. You'll find all your everyday human concerns will be met."

MATTHEW 6:30–33 MSG

The danger today is the same as it's always been: that we are so preoccupied with selfish details, we miss the wonders God has for us.

What's the answer? Jesus tells us to steep our lives in God's reality, in what God is doing, and in His blessings. Then we will have a realistic picture of the world and our place in it.

- Switch off your social media apps for a period of time each day. Use that time to interact with others face-to-face.
- Set aside time each week to enjoy God and His blessings, without interruption if possible.

Followers of Jesus will not miss out.

30. Connectivity

Nowadays, we depend on wireless services to keep us connected—through our phones, tablets, laptops and computers. Wi-Fi works along the same principles as the radio. There is a transmitter (the router) which obtains the internet information through a telephone line and sends it out via radio waves to the receiver (the Wi-Fi card in your device).

The router sends out signals in all directions at a constant intensity. The receiver in your device will only receive the signal if:

o   It is close enough to the router;
o   It is oriented to receive waves of the correct frequency;
o   It is set to the specific channel (you enter this as the "Wi-Fi Code");
o   There isn't too much interference between the router and your device, such as a thick wall or dense material;
o   There aren't too many distractions to the signal (older microwave ovens sometimes interfere with Wi-Fi signals).

In the same way, God sends His love and generosity in all directions at a constant intensity. We will only be able to access this efficiently if:

o   We stay close to God. "But as for me, it is good to be near God" (PSALM 73:28).

o We are oriented toward God. "Look to the LORD and his strength; seek his face always" (PSALM 105:4).

o We are set to receive God's message. "Do not conform to the pattern of this world, but be transformed by the renewing of your mind" (ROMANS 12:2).

o We remove interferences. "The seed falling among the thorns refers to someone who hears the word, but the worries of this life and the deceitfulness of wealth choke the word, making it unfruitful" (MATTHEW 13:22).

o We remove distractions. "Martha was distracted by all the preparations that had to be made. . . . 'Martha, Martha,' the Lord answered, 'you are worried and upset about many things, but few things are needed—or indeed only one' " (LUKE 10:40–41).

• Today, instead of worrying about being generous, focus on being close to God.
• Make sure you have time each day to remove all distractions and just sit with the Lord.

Stay connected to God's love.

31. A Double Portion

In ancient Jewish culture, the firstborn son received the largest share of the inheritance. Not just the largest share, but double that of the other sons. "When he divides his property and gives his sons their inheritances, he must recognize his true firstborn . . . and give him a double portion of all his property as is customary for all men" (DEUTERONOMY 21:16–17 THE VOICE).

This custom of giving a "double portion" was also used to show love, generosity, and blessing. Elkanah had two wives: Peninnah, who bore him many children, and Hannah, who was barren. He was generous to them all, giving them portions of his wealth. "But to Hannah he gave a double portion because he loved her" (1 SAMUEL 1:5).

Elisha was chosen by God to take over from Elijah as prophet for the nation of Israel, but he felt inadequate. "When they had crossed, Elijah said to Elisha, 'Tell me, what can I do for you before I am taken from you?' 'Let me inherit a double portion of your spirit,' Elisha replied" (2 KINGS 2:9). The subsequent story of Elisha shows that he indeed received that double portion and was able to prophesy powerfully.

Isaiah describes God's generosity to the nation of Israel even after they had wandered away from Him. "Instead of your shame you will receive a double portion . . . and everlasting joy will be yours" (ISAIAH 61:7). This is the chapter of Isaiah that Jesus read from when he first preached in Nazareth and proclaimed "the year of the Lord's favor" (LUKE 4:19).

When we follow Jesus, we are adopted as children into God's family. Jesus is the firstborn Son, the One who by rights should inherit the double portion of all that God has. But by His grace, He makes us co-heirs together with Jesus. By His generosity, we get to share fully in the inheritance. What an unimaginable blessing!

The Spirit you received brought about your adoption to sonship. And by him we cry, "Abba, Father." The Spirit himself testifies with our spirit that we are God's children. Now if we are children, then we are heirs—heirs of God and co-heirs with Christ, if indeed we share in his sufferings in order that we may also share in his glory.

ROMANS 8:15–17

- Encourage a fellow believer who is going through a rough time that they, too, are co-heirs with Christ, and that their future inheritance is secured.
- Let your generosity reflect your privileged position as a co-heir with Christ.

You can never exhaust the resources of your "double portion."

Special Occasions

New Year's Day: Heart Muscle

And now, brothers and sisters, we want you to know about the grace that God has given the Macedonian churches. In the midst of a very severe trial, their overflowing joy and their extreme poverty welled up in rich generosity. For I testify that they gave as much as they were able, and even beyond their ability.

2 CORINTHIANS 8:1–3

The New Year is often a time to make resolutions to improve in some way. Many people resolve to become fitter. They embark on a program of exercise. Some stick with it and achieve their goals; many more give up quickly.

Those who persevere often start slowly, building up stamina. Those who start with too much exercise too soon find they can't keep it up, or worse, they injure themselves because their muscles aren't used to it.

The heart is a muscle that needs exercise, not only physically but also spiritually. If we're not used to being generous, we need to start slowly and build up our "generosity" heart muscle, just as most exercise programs begin with a series of stretches in preparation for a workout. We need to stretch our spiritual heart regularly to keep it in shape, strengthening our faith as we become more and more generous over time.

Sometimes we hear about the great givers in Scripture— Abraham (HEBREWS 7:1–10), Zacchaeus (LUKE 19), the widow with her mite (LUKE 21:1–4), the Macedonian

76

church (2 CORINTHIANS 8:1–7)—and these Olympic-level examples of generosity can make us feel inadequate. We must keep in mind that we are not all called to be Olympians, but we are all called to exercise and keep fit.

So allow your heart muscle to be stretched, gently at first and then more vigorously, as God increases your faith.

- Humbly acknowledge your weak heart muscle and prepare to have it stretched.
- Be open to new opportunities to be generous, and exercise your generosity muscles every day.

Our gracious God calls us to a generosity that doesn't tear us but allows us to be stretched.

Easter Generosity

A good friend of mine had his retirement all planned out. He and his wife had bought the house of their dreams—nothing huge or fancy, but a little love nest that they were fixing up exactly the way they wanted. He was just about to sell his business, which would provide them with a comfortable retirement income, when his wife, the love of his life, suddenly died. He was forced to give up the house, and his carefully constructed vision of how he would spend the rest of his life fell apart.

Christ's resurrection from the dead is the pivotal event in all of history. It was God's most generous gift to us, and the point at which everything changed. Listen to how St. Paul describes it:

If Christ weren't raised, then all you're doing is wandering about in the dark, as lost as ever. . . . If all we get out of Christ is a little inspiration for a few short years, we're a pretty sorry lot. But the truth is that Christ has been raised up, the first in a long legacy of those who are going to leave the cemeteries. . . . In the resurrection scheme of things, this has to happen: everything perishable taken off the shelves and replaced by the imperishable, this mortal replaced by the immortal. Then the saying will come true:

Death swallowed by triumphant Life!
Who got the last word, oh, Death?
Oh, Death, who's afraid of you now?

It was sin that made death so frightening and law-code guilt that gave sin its leverage, its destructive power. But now in a single victorious stroke of Life, all three—sin, guilt, death—are gone, the gift of our Master, Jesus Christ. Thank God!

With all this going for us, my dear, dear friends, stand your ground. And don't hold back. Throw yourselves into the work of the Master, confident that nothing you do for him is a waste of time or effort.

1 CORINTHIANS 15:17, 19–20, 53–58 MSG

God has been overwhelmingly generous to us; He's released us from sin and guilt, and He will give us immortal bodies to replace our mortal ones. Christ's resurrection proves that He will.

Houses, businesses, and pension plans are short-term investments that may or may not work out. What better long-term investment, for our resources, than the kingdom of God? It is, after all, where we will spend eternity.

- Resurrect a friendship and send Easter greetings to someone you haven't been in touch with for a while.
- Invest in God's kingdom by giving an extra donation this Easter.

The Resurrection is the greatest act of generosity in history.

Harvest: Fill Your Barns

And Jesus told them this parable: "The ground of a certain rich man yielded an abundant harvest. He thought to himself, 'What shall I do? I have no place to store my crops.'

"Then he said, 'This is what I'll do. I will tear down my barns and build bigger ones, and there I will store my surplus grain. And I'll say to myself, "You have plenty of grain laid up for many years. Take life easy; eat, drink and be merry."'

"But God said to him, 'You fool! This very night your life will be demanded from you. Then who will get what you have prepared for yourself?'

"This is how it will be with whoever stores up things for themselves but is not rich toward God."

LUKE 12:16–21

Was Jesus saying that we should never enjoy abundance? Should we never save or think about the future?

I don't think this was Jesus's point. Of course it is good to plan for the future, to save for a car, a house, or for retirement. In fact, Proverbs 21:20 says, "The wise store up choice food and olive oil, but fools gulp theirs down."

Jesus was talking about hoarding, about saving simply for saving's sake, and putting your trust in that savings. The rich fool filled his barns with self, not with God. Our trust should be wholly in God, who owns the resources of the universe and is eternally more reliable than any savings plan.

The important thing is our attitude. If we are blessed with an abundance of resources, regular giving helps us keep our focus in the right place. Bringing an offering to God, in proportion to our resources, ensures that our hearts are bound to His priorities instead of material wealth.

And if we experience lean times, that attitude helps us continue trusting in God.

"Do not be afraid, little flock, for your Father has been pleased to give you the kingdom. Sell your possessions and give to the poor. Provide purses for yourselves that will not wear out, a treasure in heaven that will never fail, where no thief comes near and no moth destroys. For where your treasure is, there your heart will be also."

LUKE 12:32–34

- Review your current financial situation and your regular giving. Are they in line?
- Ask God to help you trust Him with any monetary worries you are experiencing.

Fill your barns with thankfulness to God.

Thanksgiving

"We gather together to ask the Lord's blessing . . ." We like to sing this hymn at Harvest or Thanksgiving celebrations, to thank the Lord for His generous blessings to us. The original lyrics were written by a Dutchman in 1598, thanking God for the increasing religious freedoms in that part of the world that allowed people to worship God as they saw fit. Those of us who are able to worship freely as we choose have much to be thankful for.

Whether we are directly involved in producing food from the land or pick up our food from the supermarket down the street, a Harvest or Thanksgiving service is a chance to remember our blessings. We gather together not just to sing songs but to share the bounty of those first fruits that God has entrusted to us.

Living in the central valley of California, I have done my share of fruit picking over the years. As a young man, I spent many hours climbing up ladders balanced against fruit trees. One particular pleasure was climbing up to reach the top of the peach tree. I took great satisfaction in finding the ripest peach, the one touched by the most sun, and I'd tuck it away to have for lunch. It represented the best of the first fruits.

Being part of the harvest is deeply satisfying. There is a lot of joy in gathering in the first fruits. And the joy is enhanced by giving God a portion of the harvest.

However you "gather in," whether from the soil or from a bank transfer, offer to God a portion of your blessings and experience the joy of giving your best to Him.

Honor the LORD with your wealth, with the firstfruits of all your crops; then your barns will be filled to overflowing, and your vats will brim over with new wine.

PROVERBS 3:9–10

- Think about how you "gather in," and thank God for His blessings.
- How will you honor the Lord with your firstfruits? How will you give Him an offering from your best? Make your giving a celebration!

Joy comes when we give God the best we can offer.

Christmas Anticipation

Every good present and every perfect gift comes from above, from the Father who made the sun, moon, and stars.

JAMES 1:17 GW

Do you remember as a young child the delightful anguish of waiting to open your presents on your birthday or at Christmas? In my house, my parents seemed to take pleasure in torturing us children on Christmas Day with an extra carol or an extra passage of Scripture just to prolong the exquisite agony of anticipation. Even as a child, I enjoyed the lead-up to Christmas almost as much as opening the presents themselves.

And when you start buying presents for others, there is the anticipation of the recipient's pleasure; the excitement of seeing someone open what you have taken time and trouble preparing. With the passing of years, this has become for me the primary joy of the Christmas gift exchange.

We are trustees of the bounty that God has given us. He delights in giving us good gifts and takes pleasure in our joy at receiving them. When we give an offering to God, we can give with joy, anticipating the pleasure it brings Him.

Let us give thanks all the time to God through Jesus Christ. Our gift to Him is to give thanks. Our lips should always give thanks to His name. Remember to do good and help each other. Gifts like this please God.

HEBREWS 13:15–16 NLV

- Take five minutes to step outside today and thank God for His gifts—of the world and creation, of community and friendship, of life and breath.
- The next time you give an offering, whether a special Christmas donation or just a helping hand to a neighbor, take pleasure in knowing what joy it brings to the Lord.

God takes such delight in your generosity.

- *If you enjoyed this book:* please leave a review on www.amazon.com or www.amazon.co.uk

- *If you would like to see another book in the 'Steps Toward' series:* please contact us at sjsalisbury@outlook.com

Thank you!

Permissions

Quotation that appears in "Tithing and Financial Health" (page 12) is taken from Brian Kluth, *20 Truths about Tithers Research*, www.StateofthePlate.info, 2013. Used by permission.

Poem that appears in "Do Not Judge" (page 26) was taken from www.precious-testimonies.com, written by David J Nixon, "Judge Not," 1996.

Quotation that appears in "God's Handiwork" (page 42) is an excerpt from A SHORT HISTORY OF NEARLY EVERYTHING by Bill Bryson, Copyright © 2003 Bill Bryson. Used by permission of Broadway Books, an imprint of Random House, a division of Penguin Random House LLC. All rights reserved.
Reprinted by permission of Anchor Canada/Doubleday Canada, a division of Penguin Random House Canada Limited. All rights reserved. Any third party use of this material, outside of this publication, is prohibited. Interested parties must apply directly to Penguin Random House Canada Limited for permission.

Unless otherwise noted, all Scripture quotations are taken from the HOLY BIBLE, NEW INTERNATIONAL VERSION®. NIV®. Copyright © 1973, 1978, 1984, 2011 by Biblica, Inc.™ Used by permission. All rights reserved worldwide.

Scripture quotations marked MSG are taken from THE MESSAGE, copyright © 1993, 1994, 1995, 1996, 2000, 2001, 2002 by Eugene H. Peterson. Used by permission

www.ingramcontent.com/pod-product-compliance
Lightning Source LLC
Chambersburg PA
CBHW071831020426
42331CB00007B/1684